AMERICAN HEROES

DAVID CROCKETT
Fearless Frontiersman

AMERICAN HEROES

DAVID CROCKETT
Fearless Frontiersman

SNEED B. COLLARD III

Marshall Cavendish
Benchmark
New York

For Susan Conrad,
who remembers the Alamo—and friendship, besides!

Marshall Cavendish Benchmark
99 White Plains Road
Tarrytown, New York 10591-9001
www.marshallcavendish.us

Library of Congress Cataloging-in-Publication Data
Collard, Sneed B.
David Crockett : fearless frontiersman / by Sneed B. Collard III.
p. cm. — (American heroes)
Summary: "A juvenile biography of the famous 19th-century frontiersman, politician, and Alamo defender"
—Provided by publisher. Includes bibliographical references and index.
ISBN-13: 978-0-7614-2160-3
ISBN-10: 0-7614-2160-2
1. Crockett, Davy, 1786–1836—Juvenile literature. 2. Pioneers—Tennessee—Biography—Juvenile literature.
3. Frontier and pioneer life—Tennessee—Juvenile literature. 4. Tennessee—Biography—Juvenile literature.
5. Legislators—United States—Biography—Juvenile literature. 6. United States. Congress.
House—Biography—Juvenile literature. 7. Alamo (San Antonio, Tex.)—Siege, 1836—Juvenile literature. I. Title.
F436.C95C65 2006
976.8´04092—dc22   2005037556

Editor: Joyce Stanton
Editorial Director: Michelle Bisson
Art Director: Anahid Hamparian
Series Designer and Compositor: Anne Scatto / Pixel Press
Printed in Malaysia
1 3 5 6 4 2

Images provided by Rose Corbett Gordon, Art Editor,
Mystic, CT, from the following sources:
Front cover: Burstein Collection/Corbis
Back cover: The Art Archive/Joseph Martin
Page i: Burstein Collection/Corbis; Getty Images;
pages ii , 15, 27: Bettmann/Corbis;
pages vi. 8: Private Collection/Bridgeman Art Library;
pages vii, 3, 12, 16, 19, 20, 24, 28: The Granger
Collection, NY; *page 4:* Corbis; *page 7:* The Art Archive/
Culver Pictures; *page 11:* Museum of the City of New
York, USA/The Bridgeman Art Library;
page 23: New-York Historical Society, New York/
Bridgeman Art Library; *page 31:* Hulton Archive/Getty
Images; *page 32:* The Art Archive/Joseph Martin;
page 34: National Portrait Gallery, Smithsonian
Institution/Art Resource, NY

CONTENTS

In the early 1800s, many Americans made
new lives in the western wilderness.

David Crockett

In the early 1800s, Americans were moving. From the eastern United States, they went west into the wilderness. They were settling the frontier. They cleared forests. They started new farms. These people weren't educated or rich. They were tough, down-to-earth, and very poor. They looked for a hero all their own. They found one, too. His name was David, or "Davy," Crockett.

David Crockett was born on August 17, 1786, in what is now Tennessee. David's father, John, had a hard time making a living. He tried his hand at farming. He built a mill. He even ran a tavern. But he didn't earn much money. "As a child," David later wrote, "I began to [meet] with hard times, and a plenty of them."

*When David Crockett was a boy, his father tried his hand at farming
and other activities. He met with little luck.*

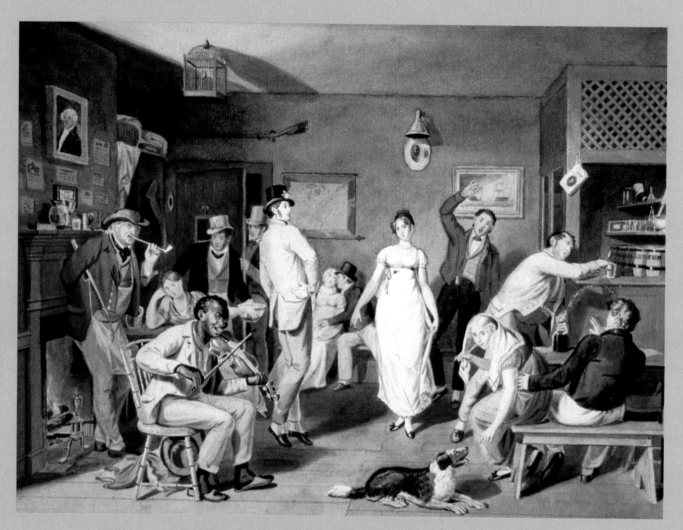

In his father's tavern, David learned to "spin" a good story.

By the time he was ten years old, David had to pitch in. He split wood for fences. He also helped drive a herd of cows more than two hundred miles away to Virginia. David gave the money he earned to his father.

But David was learning about life. He became an expert hunter. In his father's tavern, David listened to men tell wonderful stories of adventure. Soon, David could "spin" a good story himself.

When he was thirteen years old, David went to school for the first time. It lasted only four days. Right away, David got into a fight with the school bully. Afraid of being punished, he began skipping class. His father learned what his son had done. "I knew very well that I was in a devil of a hobble," David later wrote. Instead of facing a beating, David fled.

David didn't last long in school. After only four days,
he left school—and home.

On his own, David worked hard.
His honesty and hard work won him many friends.

For the next three years, David wandered from place to place. He did all kinds of jobs. He drove herds of cattle. He even found work as a hatmaker. David's honesty and friendliness made many people want to help him. By the time he returned home, David was a man. He began to plan his own future.

David knew that he needed an education to be successful in life. He had no money, so he began working for a schoolteacher in exchange for lessons. During the next six months, David learned the alphabet and how to read and write. He studied basic addition and multiplication. He also learned a bit about history, geography, art, and music.

David knew that he needed an education to succeed. He found a schoolteacher to help him learn how to read and write.

David's wife, Polly, was one of many frontier pioneers who died of disease. She left David alone with their three children.

When he was twenty years old, David met Polly Finley. They fell in love and got married. They had two sons and a daughter. But life threw many stones in David's path. In 1813 David left his family to fight the Creek Indians. Soon after he returned home, about two years later, his wife Polly died of an unknown disease. David remarried, but then he came down with malaria and almost died himself.

David's luck was about to change, however. In 1817, he moved his family to Lawrence County, Tennessee. Here, politics caught his interest. His neighbors chose him to be a justice of the peace. A few years later, David became a candidate for the state assembly.

Voters liked David's friendly face and lively storytelling. They also laughed at his tricks. One day, David and another candidate went to a big election rally. David spoke first. When he finished his speech, he invited everyone to go drink whiskey with him. They did, and the other candidate never got a chance to speak! David easily won the election.

Storytelling and a sense of humor helped make David a natural politician.

David's skills as a hunter won him a lot of votes.

As an assemblyman, David tried to help other poor people like himself. He supported forming a state bank that would loan money to farmers. That way, they could buy their own land. When he wasn't serving the public, David headed into the wilderness. With a tomahawk and butcher knife at his side, he stalked prey through the forest. In just one spring, David wrote, "I killed ten bears, and a great abundance of deer." His image as a rugged frontiersman began to grow.

David's star kept rising. In 1827, he was elected to the United States Congress. In 1833, a popular new book and play about him appeared. These works showed "Davy" Crockett as a fearless pioneer who could whip his weight in wildcats. They said he was "half-horse, half-alligator, a little touched with snapping turtle."

"Half-horse and half-alligator," David was elected
to the U.S. Congress in 1827.

In Congress, David was as honest and independent as he was on the frontier.

Much of what was written about David was not true. In fact, David never even called himself "Davy." No one cared. To ordinary Americans, David had become a hero. He had all of the qualities they valued—honesty, courage, humor, and independence. People even talked about him becoming president of the United States!

But David had enemies, too. As a congressman, David never learned to work with other politicians to get things done. He lost his next election. Overnight, all talk of his becoming president melted away.

Sad and defeated, David realized there was little left for him in Tennessee. His second marriage had fallen apart. He also owed a lot of money to people. He decided to try someplace new.

With little left for him in Tennessee,
David decided to try someplace new.

*Texas was a wide-open country where both
Mexicans and Americans lived.*

All this time, David had been hearing wonderful things about Texas. This big new territory in the West belonged to Mexico. It had rich farmland and a wide-open frontier—just the kind of place for a man who needed a fresh start.

What David didn't realize was that Texas was having its own problems.

For several years Americans had been flooding into Texas. By 1835, these Americans, along with some Mexicans, wanted Texas to become its own country.

Soon, war broke out. Mexico's ruler, Santa Anna, led an army north to crush the revolt. He marched toward the city of San Antonio.

In San Antonio, a ragtag group of about 150 Texan soldiers prepared to defend themselves. Their headquarters was an old mission called the Alamo. The soldiers were tired. They were short of food. Worse, it didn't look like anyone was coming to help them.

The Mexican ruler Santa Anna led his army north to crush the Texas revolt.

When he heard about the men at the Alamo,
David Crockett decided to help.

Then, early in February 1836, a man from Tennessee suddenly appeared. It was David Crockett. David hadn't set out for Texas looking to fight. But when he heard about the men defending the Alamo, he decided he had to help. He announced, "Me and my Tennessee boys have come to help Texas."

David brought only a few men with him. But his stories and eagerness cheered the Texan troops. They even threw a party in David's honor.

Toward the end of February, Santa Anna arrived. Four thousand Mexican troops surrounded the Alamo. David quickly proved his courage. During one battle, he raced everywhere, urging the Texans to fight. With his own rifle, he helped drive back the Mexicans.

But the Mexicans did not give up. Before dawn on March 6, Santa Anna attacked again. David and his men defended the weakest part of the Alamo, but there were too many enemy soldiers. By sunrise, Santa Anna's army had killed every last man in the Alamo.

With his own rifle, David helped drive back
the Mexican soldiers.

David Crockett's bravery at the Alamo helped make him a lasting American hero.

No one is exactly sure how David Crockett died. Some say he was killed inside the Alamo. Many think he was caught and killed later by Santa Anna. No one will ever know for sure.

But the courage David and the Texans showed at the Alamo will never be forgotten. Because of the Alamo, Texans continued to fight for, and win, their independence from Mexico. Later, Texas became part of the United States.

David Crockett spent only a few days in Texas. But those few days—along with his honesty, courage, humor, and independence—placed him in the hearts of all Americans forever.

IMPORTANT DATES

1786 Born on August 17 near what is now Limestone, Tennessee.

1795 David's parents move the family to near what is now Morristown, Tennessee. His father John opens a tavern.

1798 Hired to help drive cattle more than two hundred miles to Virginia.

1799 Runs away from home for three years; works at a variety of jobs.

1806 Marries Polly Finley.

1813–1815 Fights the Creek Indians as part of the War of 1812.

1815 Wife Polly dies.

1816 Marries Elizabeth Patton.

1817 Moves family to Lawrence County, Tennessee; chosen as justice of the peace.

1821 Elected to state assembly.

1827 Elected as member of the United States Congress.

1833 A popular book and play help make David a hero.

1834 Publishes his own book, *A Narrative of the Life of David Crockett,* leading to even greater fame.

1835 Defeated in reelection bid for Congress; decides to leave the United States for Texas.

1836 Dies on March 6 defending the Alamo against Mexican forces.

Words to Know

assemblyman A person who serves in a state assembly.

candidate Someone who is running for a public office, such as mayor, congressman, or president.

congressman A person who serves in the United States Congress.

Creek Indians An Indian nation that lived in the southeastern United States.

frontier The far edge of a country, where people are just beginning to settle.

independence Freedom.

justice of the peace A local judge who handles small legal cases and can also perform marriages and other ceremonies.

malaria A disease spread by mosquitoes. It causes chills and fever and often kills its victims.

politician A person who is, or works to be, elected to public office.

rally An event where candidates for public office tell people why they should be elected.

revolt An uprising against a government.

state assembly A branch of a state government made up of people who are elected from different parts of the state. These representatives help pass laws, create budgets, and make other decisions on how a state is run.

tavern A small bar or inn where alcoholic beverages are served.

United States Congress A branch of the government made up of people who are elected from all of the fifty states. Like a state assembly, the Congress creates laws and decides how the government is run.

War of 1812 A war fought between the United States and Great Britain between 1812 and 1815. In this war, the Creek Indians sided with Great Britain to fight against the United States.

To Learn More about David Crockett

WEB SITES

The Alamo
   http://www.thealamo.org
American West: A Celebration of the Human Spirit
   http://www.americanwest.com/pages/davycroc.htm

BOOKS

The Alamo by Mary Ann Noonan Guerra. The Alamo Press, 1996.

Davy Crockett by Elaine Marie Alphin. Lerner Books, 2002.

Davy Crockett by David A. Adler. Heinemann, 2003.

A Picture Book of Davy Crockett by David Adler. Holiday House, 1998.

Voices of the Alamo by Sherry Garland. Scholastic, 2000.

PLACES TO VISIT

The Alamo
300 Alamo Plaza, P.O. Box 2599
San Antonio, Texas 78299
PHONE: (210) 225-1391   WEB SITE: **www.thealamo.org**

Crockett Tavern Museum
2002 Morningside Drive
Morristown, Tennessee 37814
PHONE: (423) 587-9900   WEB SITE: **www.discoveret.org/crockett**

Davy Crockett Birthplace State Park
1245 Davy Crockett Park Road
Limestone, Tennessee 37681
PHONE: (423) 257-2167
WEB SITE:
www.state.tn.us/environment/parks/parks/DavyCrockettSHP

INDEX

Page numbers for illustrations are in boldface.

ABOUT THE AUTHOR

SNEED B. COLLARD III is the author of more than fifty award-winning books for young people, including *The Prairie Builders*; *A Platypus, Probably*; *One Night in the Coral Sea*; and the four-book SCIENCE ADVENTURES series for Marshall Cavendish Benchmark. In addition to his writing, Sneed is a popular speaker and presents widely to students, teachers, and the general public. In 2006, he was selected as the Washington Post–Children's Book Guild Nonfiction Award winner for his achievements in children's writing. He is also the author of several novels for young adults, including *Dog Sense* and *Flash Point*. To learn more about Sneed, visit his Web site at www.sneedbcollardiii.com.